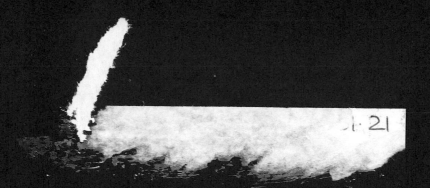

VOLCANOES

Jane Walker

GLOUCESTER PRESS
LONDON · NEW YORK · SYDNEY

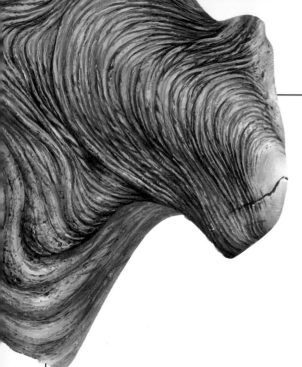

INTRODUCTION

When a volcano erupts, it is one of Nature's most powerful forces. In this book we find out how volcanoes are formed, and what makes them erupt. We look at some of the world's most famous volcanoes, and learn about the damage they have caused. You can have fun with **Practical Projects,** a **Volcanic Quiz**, and discover a lot of **Amazing Facts** about volcanoes.

© Aladdin Books Ltd 1994

Designed and produced by
Aladdin Books Ltd
28 Percy Street
London W1P 9FF

First published in
Great Britain in 1994 by
WATTS BOOKS
96 Leonard Street
London EC2A 4RH

Design: David West
             Children's Book
             Design
Designer: Flick Killerby
Editors: Angela Travis
             Richard Green
Illustrators: Mike Saunders
             Peter Kesteven
Cartoons: Tony Kenyon
Consultant: Joyce Pope

ISBN 0 7496 1164 2

Printed in Belgium
A CIP catalogue record
for this book is available
from the British Library

CONTENTS

INSIDE THE EARTH

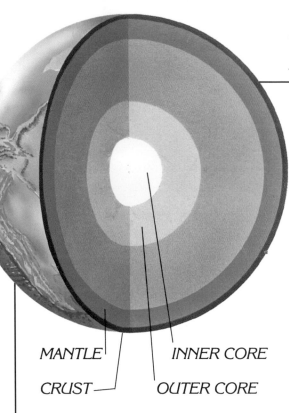

MANTLE

CRUST

INNER CORE

OUTER CORE

The Earth's layers
The Earth is not solid right through to its centre. Below the crust is another layer of hard rocks, called the mantle. Beneath the mantle is the outer core, which is made of hot rocks. It is so hot in the outer core that the rocks melt and turn into a liquid. At the centre of the Earth is the inner core. The temperature here is about 5,000 degrees centigrade, but because of a force called pressure the inner core is solid metal.

The surface of the Earth is covered with either land or water. Beneath the land and the oceans is a layer of rocky material. This layer surrounds the whole Earth and is called the Earth's crust. Although it seems to be hard and solid, the crust is really only a thin outer shell. Below the land, the crust is between 32 and 40 kilometres thick but only eight kilometres thick under the oceans.

A god called Vulcan

Volcanoes are named after Vulcan, the Roman god of fire. Vulcan was also the blacksmith for the gods, making their arrows, spears and other weapons. The Romans believed that Vulcan worked in a forge under the volcanic island of Vulcano in the Mediterranean Sea. They thought that when Vulcan was hammering and striking metal in his forge, he made the volcano erupt, sending out showers of lava and hot ash.

The CASCADE MOUNTAINS run down the west coast of the USA. There are several active volcanoes in this mountain range, including Mount St Helens.

What is a volcano?

In places where the Earth's crust is weak, holes or cracks appear. When magma (hot, liquid rocks deep below the crust) travels upwards through the mantle and bursts through one of these weak spots, a volcano forms.

MOVING CONTINENTS

All the separate areas of land on Earth once formed one huge continent called Pangaea. Slowly, over millions of years, Pangaea began to break up. The drifting areas of land eventually settled into the positions of the seven continents in the world as it is today.

The beginning of the EARTH

EARTH 50 million years ago

EARTH 150 million years ago

The Earth's plates

Scientists believe that the Earth's crust is divided into separate sections, called plates. The plates are like floating rafts moving on the layer of soft rocks beneath them. The continents and the ocean-floors are carried by these plates. Today, scientists think that the Earth's surface can be divided into about 15 separate plates.

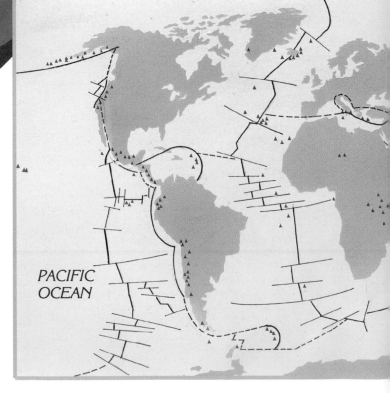

PACIFIC OCEAN

Fiery beginnings

About 4,500 million years ago, the planet Earth was formed from a spinning cloud of hot dust and gas. Its surface was molten until 4,000 million years ago when it began to harden into a rocky crust with thousands of volcanoes.

EARTH today

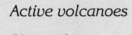
▲ *Active volcanoes*
╲ *Plate edges*

PACIFIC OCEAN

The Ring of Fire

The Earth's crust is weaker at the edges of the plates (where two different plates meet). Many volcanoes are found either on top of or close to these edges. Over half of the world's active volcanoes are found around the Pacific Ocean. They lie in a circle called the Ring of Fire. Volcanoes are also found in other areas at plate edges, such as the Mediterranean Sea, Iceland and across southern Europe, as well as on the floor of the Atlantic Ocean.

WHEN PLATES MOVE

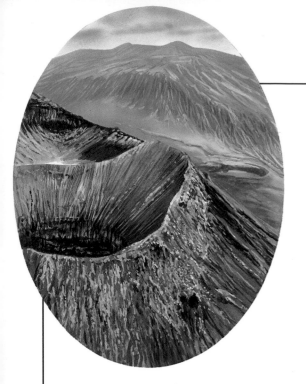

The Great Rift Valley
Some mountains and valleys formed when plates pulled apart. The Great Rift Valley (above), which runs through East Africa, was made in this way. As plates pulled apart, they left a wide valley with volcanoes at the edges.

The huge plates of the Earth's crust move all the time, not more than a few centimetres each year. Plates push against, or pull away from each other. When two plates collide, one plate may be pushed down into the mantle below the crust, where it melts. Volcanoes are found in areas where plates collide or pull apart.

When two ocean PLATES meet, one is pushed down into the mantle, leaving a deep ocean trench. This plate melts and produces molten rock which may erupt as a volcano.

When two ocean PLATES pull apart, molten material rises up and turns solid forming an ocean ridge.

Mountains

Moving plates also make some of the world's high mountains. When the plates in the Earth's crust push together, the rocks of land edges and solid parts of the ocean floor are squeezed upwards to form mountains. The Alps in Europe, the Himalayas in Asia and the Andes Mountains of South America were all made in this way.

Pressure from plate movements can cause rock layers to crack. Rift valleys, mountains and volcanoes may then occur.

MOUNTAIN chains have formed at the edges of continents where two plates have collided.

VENUS

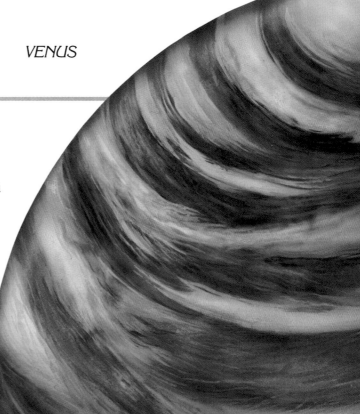

Volcanoes in space

Did you know that there are volcanoes up in space? Scientists think there are volcanoes on the planet Venus. The biggest space volcano is on Mars. It is called Olympus Mons and is over 25 kilometres high, which is more than twice the height of Mount Everest, the Earth's highest mountain.

ERUPTION!

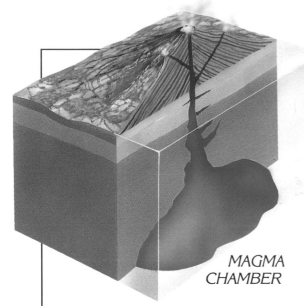

MAGMA
CHAMBER

An erupting volcano is a spectacular and frightening sight. Dust and gas shoot into the sky from the main pipe of the volcano. Streams of red-hot magma, called lava when it comes to the surface, pour from the top of the volcano and down its sides. Sometimes the gases and rocks that are trapped inside the volcano burst out with great force in a deafening explosion.

Ready to erupt

Beneath a volcano lies a large space called the magma chamber (above). Just before an eruption, the magma chamber fills with red-hot magma and the sides of the volcano may start to bulge outwards. Sometimes the ground shakes and there is a smell as gases, containing sulphur, escape from the rocks.

During a VOLCANIC ERUPTION, hot gases, steam, dust and pieces of rock shoot out of the volcano, followed by rivers of fiery lava.

LAVA FLOW

The eruption of MOUNT ST HELENS, in the USA, was as powerful as 500 atomic bombs.

Make your own volcano

On a solid base of wood or plastic, build a papier mâché cone around an old plastic mug (be careful not to cover the top of the mug). When the papier mâché is dry, make your volcano more realistic by painting it. Put one teaspoon of baking powder into the mug. Mix a few drops of red food colouring with some vinegar and pour it into the mug. A red-coloured foam will pour over the volcano's sides as it 'erupts'.

MAIN PIPE, OR VENT

After a very violent eruption, the volcano may collapse to form a huge crater, called a CALDERA.

EARTH'S CRUST

MAGMA CHAMBER

WHICH VOLCANO?

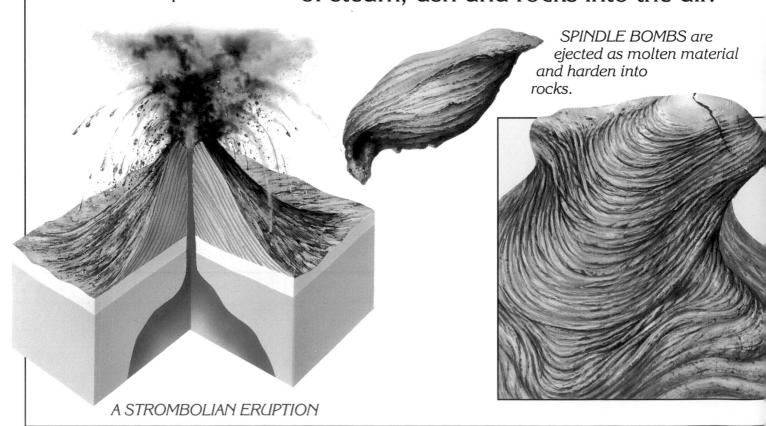

A HAWAIIAN ERUPTION

Volcanoes vary in shape and size. Many volcanoes are cone-shaped mountains, others are just long cracks in the ground. Some are quite small and steep, while others are high mountains, formed over many years from layers of lava and ash. Volcanoes also erupt differently. Some erupt quietly, without much force. Others erupt violently, sending tonnes of steam, ash and rocks into the air.

Types of eruptions

When a Hawaiian volcano erupts, dark lava pours quietly down the volcano's sides (above). In a Strombolian eruption (below), fountains of fire, steam and gas gush out of the volcano's top.

SPINDLE BOMBS are ejected as molten material and harden into rocks.

A STROMBOLIAN ERUPTION

Stopping the flow

For hundreds of years people have tried to stop the lava flows from erupting volcanoes. Over 300 years ago, the people of Sicily used iron bars to stop lava from Mount Etna reaching the ancient town of Catania. In the 1930s, American aircraft bombed the lava flow from Hawaii's Mauna Loa. Also in Hawaii, workers used bulldozers to build a huge wall of earth to protect homes from Mount Kilauea.

Houses buried in hot ash and dust from a GLOWING CLOUD

Glowing clouds

A Peléean is the most violent kind of eruption. Glowing clouds of gas, steam and rock blast out of a volcano. The thick clouds drop down onto the volcano and race down its sides. One of the largest glowing clouds ever seen came from an eruption of Mount Pelée in the Caribbean, killing 40,000 people.

VOLCANIC BLOCKS are chunks of old rock ejected as solids.

Cooled lava which feels rough and spiky is called AA (below). Smooth lava that looks like coiled-up rope is called PAHOEHOE, or ropy lava (left).

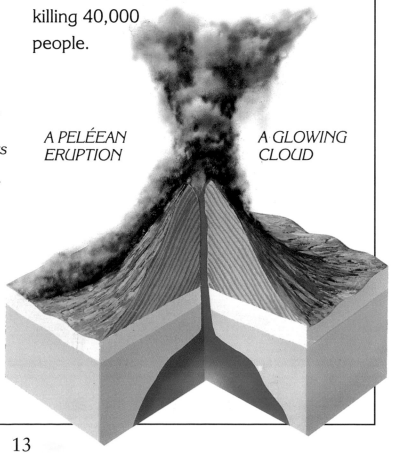

A PELÉEAN ERUPTION

A GLOWING CLOUD

EXTINCT OR ASLEEP?

Scientists at work

Teams of scientists watch how volcanoes behave. They study the lava and other materials that come from an erupting volcano. The scientist above is using a steel pipe to measure the depth of a new lava flow.

MOUNT BROMO in Java is one of the world's most active volcanoes.

Do you know that scientists describe some volcanoes as sleeping, or dormant? This means that a volcano has been quiet for a long time but there are still signs (such as bubbling lava in the crater and rising steam) that it may erupt again and become active. Of the 500 active volcanoes in the world, only 20-30 erupt each year. If there has been no sign of activity from the volcano (such as heat or steam) for a very long time, we say it is extinct.

The Giant's Causeway

The Giant's Causeway, in Northern Ireland, is an amazing area of rocky pillars made from lava. As the lava cooled, it formed a black rock, called basalt. Each pillar has six sides. According to one Irish legend, it was made by the giant Finn MacCool. He built the Causeway to reach his enemy, a giant across the sea in Scotland.

Volcanic surprises

The country of Indonesia in the Pacific Ocean has the largest number of active volcanoes. Since the early 1800s, a total of 67 volcanoes have erupted on about 600 different occasions. Scientists in the former Soviet Union were surprised when Mount Bezimiannyi suddenly erupted over 35 years ago. They believed that the volcano was extinct!

MOUNT FUJI in Japan is a dormant volcano which last erupted in 1707.

The AUVERGNE region of France has 50 extinct volcanoes. The volcanoes have not erupted for more than 6,000 years and have been eroded away, leaving plugs of unerupted hardened magma, which look like rounded hilltops.

UNDERSEA VOLCANOES

UNDERSEA VOLCANO

Undersea volcanoes form when the ocean floor moves over a very hot area in the mantle, called a hotspot. As the magma breaks through the ocean floor and cools, lava can build up and form a shield volcano. The Hawaiian islands were made this way and are shaped like the circular shields of soldiers from long ago.

Below the surface

Many undersea volcanoes lie completely hidden below the water's surface. When they erupt, the lava is instantly cooled by the sea water. It hardens into small blocks and is called pillow lava. In the Caribbean, one undersea volcano is slowly growing taller. Scientists think that it may break through the ocean's surface by the year 2000.

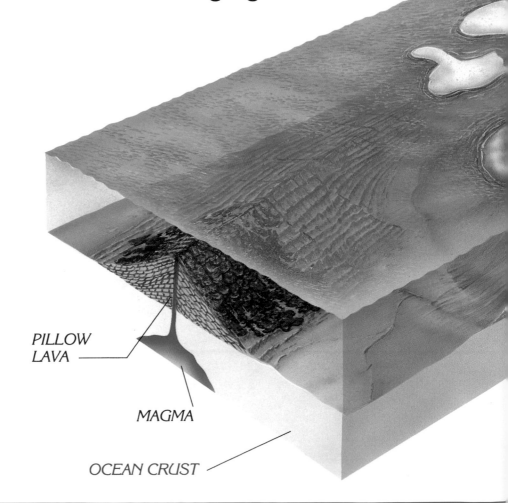

PILLOW LAVA

MAGMA

OCEAN CRUST

What is an atoll?

An atoll is a ring of coral on the rim of an extinct volcano in the sea. Tiny sea creatures, called polyps, build up the coral atolls with their hard skeletons. They settle on the rims of volcanoes which have either been worn away by the sea, or have sunk back down below the water's surface.

Life around coral

The warm waters around atolls and other kinds of coral reef are filled with colourful fish like this coral trout (above). Other sea creatures, such as starfish and sea cucumbers, feed on the tiny plants and animals that live around the coral.

The lost city of Atlantis

The ancient Greek legend of Atlantis tells of a wonderful island which mysteriously disappeared into the sea. Some scientists believe the story is about the Greek island of Santorini, which was destroyed by a huge volcanic eruption in 1470 BC.

New Volcanoes

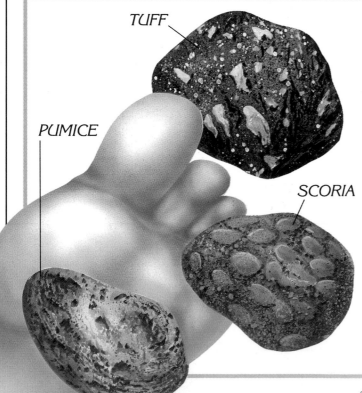

1952 – 412 metres

1944 – 335 metres

1943 – 10 metres

A Mexican surprise
In 1943, the first sign of a new volcano was white steam rising from the middle of a Mexican cornfield. The volcano, in Parícutin, grew to a height of 412 metres and erupted for nine years.

Most of the volcanoes in the world today were formed millions of years ago. But new volcanoes can still appear. On the island of Heimaey in Iceland, a new volcano appeared in January 1973, covering the island in ash or lava and forcing most of the inhabitants to leave the island. Thirty years earlier, another new volcano suddenly appeared on land – in the middle of a cornfield in Mexico!

TUFF

PUMICE

SCORIA

Volcanic rocks
The Romans used volcanic material to build parts of the city of Rome. The material, called tuff, is made from a volcano's ash and cinders. Another volcanic material is scoria, a volcanic rock containing air holes, often used to make grinding or polishing products. Pumice, a form of scoria, is a light-coloured rock that can float in water. Some people use pumice stone to clean their skin.

The PARICUTIN VOLCANO, in Mexico, grew more than 125 metres in a week.

New islands

A new volcanic island rose up out of the sea near Iceland in 1963. It was called Surtsey, after the Icelandic god of fire. A volcano on the floor of the Atlantic Ocean had started to erupt violently (1) as two plates pulled apart. Next, a tiny island broke through the surface of the ocean and grew (2). Finally, it reached more than 170 metres above the water (3).

Soon after SURTSEY appeared, plants grew as birds and winds brought seeds.

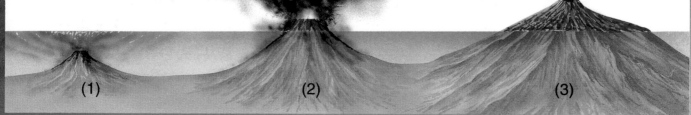

(1)   (2)   (3)

VESUVIUS

The volcano VESUVIUS erupted on 24 August AD 79.

Over 1,900 years ago, Mount Vesuvius erupted destroying the Roman towns of Pompeii and Herculaneum in southern Italy. More than 20,000 people died under piles of ash and mud. Today, tourists visit the ruins of Pompeii, where scientists have uncovered houses, animals and human bodies preserved in ash.

Making plaster casts

You can make your own plaster casts of objects such as shells or other figures. Press an object into some modelling clay to make a mould. Carefully peel away the object. Now, mix some plaster of Paris and pour it into the mould. When the plaster is dry, remove the mould to create your own plaster cast.

Life in Pompeii

The ruins of Pompeii help us to understand how Roman towns were designed, with important buildings such as the amphitheatre, the market, buildings for the government officials and bath houses. The remains have taught us about how people lived all those years ago, their everyday life, customs and how they relaxed.

The remains of POMPEII and HERCULANEUM were discovered 1,700 years after they were buried.

A mosaic picture which was uncovered in POMPEII, showing a scene from the River Nile, Egypt.

The town of POMPEII was buried under layers of ash. The ash hardened and helped to preserve much of the town and its inhabitants.

FAMOUS VOLCANOES

Some volcanoes become famous through stories and legends. Others, such as Krakatau, have caused such terrible disasters that many people have heard of them. The eruption of Mount St Helens is one of the best ever recorded. Scientists had the opportunity to study and photograph the volcano as it began to erupt.

Mount Etna

As long ago as 700 BC, people started to keep a record of how many times Mount Etna erupted. Since then the volcano, on the island of Sicily, has erupted over 250 times. In 1979 a new crater opened up without warning at the feet of tourists. Some were killed and others were injured.

Krakatau

In 1883, a volcano on the uninhabited Indonesian island of Krakatau erupted. The island of Krakatau itself was almost completely destroyed. Worse still, the eruption created an enormous tidal wave which swept onto nearby islands, killing over 35,000 people.

When KRAKATAU erupted in 1883, it was heard nearly 5,000 km away in Australia.

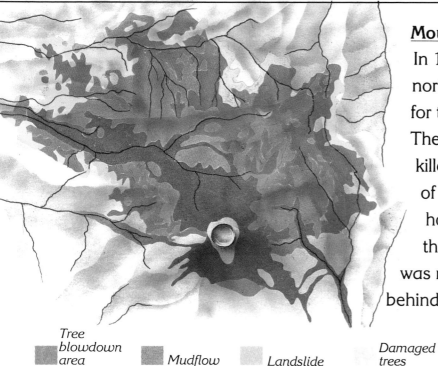

Tree blowdown area Mudflow Landslide Damaged trees New lakes

Mount St Helens

In 1980, Mount St Helens, on the north-west coast of the USA, erupted for the first time in over 120 years. The eruption was so powerful that it killed 57 people and caused millions of dollars of damage to nearby homes, roads, crops and forests. As the volcano exploded, a huge area was ripped out from its sides, leaving behind an enormous crater.

The sacred mountain

Mount Fuji is the highest and most sacred mountain in Japan. The crater of a dormant volcano lies at its top. Every summer, half a million Japanese people visit Mount Fuji. The mountain has appeared in many Japanese paintings and prints and is a popular image of Japan around the world today.

After destroying the island of KRAKATAU, the volcano continued to erupt and finally a new island, ANAK KRAKATAU (Child of Krakatau), appeared.

THE GOOD AND THE BAD

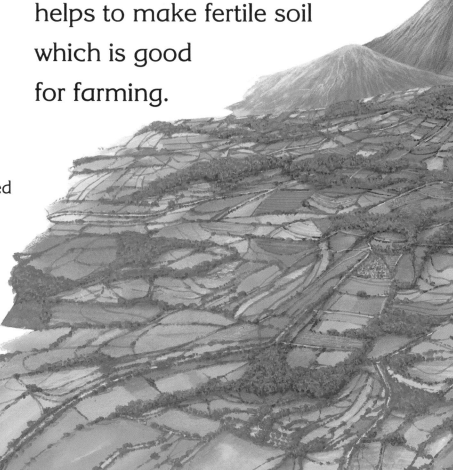

GEOTHERMAL ENERGY

Hot rocks

In countries like Iceland and New Zealand, hot rocks under the Earth heat the water underground. The heated water gives off steam which is used to make electricity. This kind of energy is called geothermal energy. It is very clean and does not pollute the environment. The heated water can also be piped into people's homes.

Although volcanoes can be very destructive, they do bring us some benefits. The different kinds of rock and lava thrown out by an erupting volcano can be used for building materials and cleaning products. Sulphur is used in certain chemicals and volcanic ash helps to make fertile soil which is good for farming.

Gems and minerals

Valuable metals and gemstones such as sapphires and zircons are often found near volcanoes. They are buried in layers of rock which formed when the liquid magma cooled and hardened. Copper, silver and gold have all been mined from volcanic rocks. Some of the biggest diamonds in the world have also come from volcanic rock. In the town of Kimberley in South Africa, diamonds were found inside a rock called kimberlite. It had been formed inside a volcano long ago.

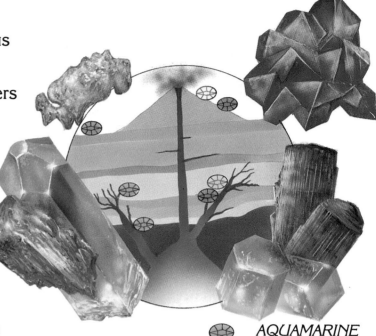

 OPAL

 ZIRCON

TOURMALINE

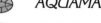 AQUAMARINE

 TOPAZ

MOONSTONE

 BERYL

Farmland

Some soils which are formed from volcanic material are very fertile. On the slopes of Mount Etna on the Mediterranean island of Sicily, groves of orange and lemon trees grow next to rows of healthy vines. The Canary Islands, off Africa's north-west coast, have several volcanic mountains. Many fruits, such as bananas, grow in the island's rich, fertile soil.

Diamonds and drills

Did you know that diamonds are used to cut other diamonds? This is because diamonds are the hardest natural materials found on Earth. They are used to cut, grind and drill. The end of a drill for cutting very hard rock is covered in tiny pointed pieces of diamond. Other drills are coated with diamond dust or diamond powder.

Volcano Relatives

Hot rocks inside the Earth heat up the steam, hot gases and lava which come out of volcanoes. These rocks also heat up the water below the Earth's surface. This hot water bubbles up to the surface where it appears as a hot spring.

One kind of hot spring which behaves a bit like a volcano is called a geyser. Geysers throw out tall jets of hot water, often with clouds of white water droplets. After an eruption, the water seeps back into the earth, leaving behind minerals. These minerals sometimes form cones which fill with wonderfully clear water between eruptions.

The Japanese city of BEPPU has over 4,000 hot springs. The water in the springs at the side of the road is hot enough to cook an egg.

"Old Faithful"

One of the world's most famous geysers is in Yellowstone National Park in the USA. The geyser is nicknamed "Old Faithful" because it erupts about once every hour. In all of the 80 years it has been observed, it has never missed an eruption and has reached a height of 46 metres.

Sometimes, the water from hot springs mixes with mud from the rocks around them and a bubbling mud pot or mud volcano forms. New Zealand, which has a number of active volcanoes, is well known for its geysers and mud pots.

The different kinds of tiny plants and animals which are able to live in the in the heat of this spring in YELLOWSTONE NATIONAL PARK, USA, create a rainbow of colours in the water.

Hot water

Some of the water below the Earth's surface is rainwater. The layers of rock soak it up like a huge sponge. Heat from the magma rises up and heats this water, which rises back to the surface as a hot spring. One kind of hot spring is really a hole in the ground that gives out a mixture of steam and other gases. It is called a fumarole, and some of the gases are quite poisonous.

FUMAROLE

MAGMA

HOT ROCKS *MUD POT*

GEYSER

HOT SPRING

MUD bubbles up from this mud pot.

OLD FAITHFUL

A Volcanic Quiz

How much do you know about volcanoes? Can you remember the names of the different kinds of volcano? And what happens to the red-hot lava when it cools down and hardens? Here is a volcano picture quiz to test how much you have learned. The picture clues should help you to find the right answers. You could try out the quiz on your friends and family. All the answers can be found on the pages of this book.

1. How many extinct volcanoes can be found in the Auvergne region of France?

2. What happens to the ocean bed when plates pull apart?

3. What is the name of this type of volcanic rock?

4. What do we call lava that hardens undersea?

5. Near which valley in East Africa can this volcano be found?

6. What can pumice stone be used for?

MORE AMAZING FACTS

Mount Erebus, in Antarctica, has ICE CHIMNEYS 20 metres high, made by fumaroles (steaming holes in the ground).

Volcanic material from the volcano on Santorini was used to build the SUEZ CANAL.

HADRIAN'S WALL in northern England is built over a ledge of rock made from cooled magma.

In 1873 the volcano MAUNA LOA began to erupt but did not stop for over one and a half years.

Japanese MACAQUE MONKEYS sit in hot water springs to keep warm in winter.

The world's tallest geyser, WAIMANGU in New Zealand, once erupted to a height of over 450 metres.

Joseph Surtout survived the MOUNT PELÉE eruption. He was locked up in a dungeon and was saved by the thickness of the walls.

A LAVA FLOW on Mount Vesuvius was recorded travelling at 80 kph.

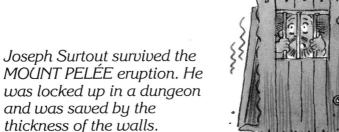

GLOSSARY

ACTIVE Describes a volcano that may still erupt.

ATOLL A ring-shaped coral island built on the top of an underwater volcano.

CRATER The top of a volcano.

CRUST The layer of hard rock that surrounds the Earth.

DORMANT Describes a volcano that has not erupted for a long time. It may erupt again one day.

ERUPT To throw out hot rocks, gases and other material through a hole in the Earth's surface.

EXTINCT Describes a volcano that has not erupted for thousands of years.

FUMAROLE A hot spring that gives off steam and other gases.

GEOTHERMAL ENERGY Energy made using underground steam. The steam can be used to produce electricity.

GEYSER A hot spring that shoots out jets of hot water and steam.

HOT SPRING A place where hot water, which has been heated inside the Earth, comes to the surface.

LAVA The hot liquid rocks that pour out of a volcano.

MAGMA Melted rock inside the Earth. When a volcano erupts magma comes to the surface and is called lava.

MAGMA CHAMBER An area filled with magma which lies beneath a volcano.

MANTLE The layer of hard rock immediately beneath the Earth's crust. Beneath the mantle, some of the rocks are liquid and move.

MUD POT A bubbling hot spring where the water has mixed with mud.

PLATE A section of the Earth's crust. There are about 15 separate plates.

PUMICE A volcanic rock that has bubbles of gas trapped inside it.

TIDAL WAVE A giant sea wave that is sometimes caused by an erupting volcano.

INDEX

A
active volcanoes 7, 14, 15
atolls 17
Auvergne 15

C
calderas 11
craters 9, 11

D
dormant volcanoes 14

E
Earth's crust 4, 5, 7, 8, 9
Earth's inner core 4
eruptions 10-13
extinct volcanoes 14, 15

F
formation of volcanoes 5
fumaroles 26, 30

G
geothermal energy 24
geysers 26, 27, 30
Giant's Causeway 15
Great Rift Valley 8

H
Hawaiian islands 13, 16

Heimaey 18
hot rocks 24, 26
hot springs 26, 30
hotspots 16

I
Indonesia 15

K
Krakatau 22-3

L
lava 10, 13, 14, 15, 16, 30
legends 5, 15, 17

M
magma 5, 10, 16, 25, 26, 30
mantle 4, 8, 16
Mauna Loa 5, 13, 30
Mount Etna 13, 22, 25
Mount Fuji 15, 23
Mount Pelee 13, 30
Mount St Helens 11, 22, 23
Mount Vesuvius 20-1, 30
mountains 5, 9
mud pots 27

N
New Volcanoes 18-19

O
"Old Faithful" 27
Olympus Mons 9

P
Parícutin 18, 19
plates 6, 7, 8, 9
Pompeii 20-1

R
Ring of Fire 7

S
scientific studies 14, 22
shield volcanoes 16
space volcanoes 9
Surtsey 19

U
undersea volcanoes 16-19,

V
volcanic ash 24
volcanic material 10, 24, 25, 30
volcanic rock 12, 15, 18

PHOTOCREDITS

Cover and pages 5 and 17: Mary Evans Picture Library.